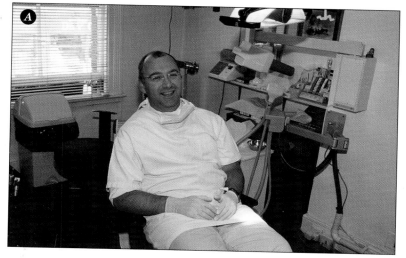

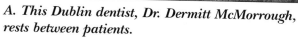

A. This Dublin dentist, Dr. Dermitt McMorrough, rests between patients.

B. These school girls pass through a Belfast neighborhood on their way home.

C. In Ireland's countryside, horses are a popular way to get around. The road sign is in both English and Irish Gaelic.

D. An Irish fry, or breakfast, is served by a Dublin waiter.

E. The Irish are very superstitious about weddings. If a bride tears her wedding dress, it is considered gook luck.

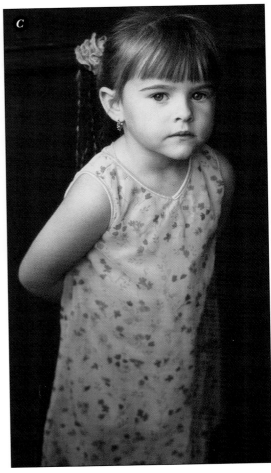

A. *These boys practice their aerial jumps in the school parking lot.*

B. *After school, skateboarding is a popular way to have fun.*

C. *Siobhan is looking for her mother.*

IRELAND
the people

Erinn Banting

A Bobbie Kalman Book
The Lands, Peoples, and Cultures Series

Crabtree Publishing Company
www.crabtreebooks.com

The Lands, Peoples, and Cultures Series

Created by Bobbie Kalman

Coordinating editor
Ellen Rodger

Project editor
P.A. Finlay

Production coordinator
Rosie Gowsell

Project development, photo research, and design
First Folio Resource Group, Inc.
Erinn Banting
Tom Dart
Greg Duhaney
Söğüt Y. Güleç
Debbie Smith

Editing
Carolyn Black

Prepress and printing
Worzalla Publishing Company

Consultants
Brian Costello; Dissolving Boundaries Through Technology in Education; Stephen Guidon; Matthew Keenan; Darren Kenny; Sean MacMathuna; Michael J. McCann, InfoMarex; Liam Merwick; Jennifer O'Connell and North Dublin National School Project's 5th class; Michael O'Gorman; Paul Quinn; Chris Stephenson; Colin Stephenson

Special Thanks
Thanks to Ivoane McMorough who connected us with her wonderful friends in Ireland. Thanks to Patrick and Creena MacNiell who passed their love for Ireland on to Crabtree Publishing. Thanks to Oliver Cooney, Principal of St. Michael's School, Ratharolyon, Republic of Ireland; Niall Moynihan, Deputy Principal, St. Michael's School and the students of St. Michael's School; Dr. Dermitt McMorrough; Anne Cooney; Gerry Gallivan; Brian and Barbara Gallivan and family.

Photographs
Corbis/ Magma Photo News Inc./Tony Arru: p. 25; Corbis/Magma Photo News Inc./Bettmann: p. 13 (left); Corbis/ Magma Photo News Inc./Annie Griffiths Belt: p. 20 (left); Corbis/Magma Photo News Inc./Becky Luigart-Stayner: p. 24 (right); Corbis/Magma Photo News Inc./David Muench: p. 3; Corbis/Magma Photo News Inc./Michael St. Maur Sheil: p. 13 (right), p. 29 (top); Corbis/Magma Photo News Inc./Geray Sweeney: p. 22 (bottom); Corbis/Magma Photo News Inc./David and Peter Turnley: p. 21; Courau/Explorer/ Photo Researchers: p. 16 (top); Marc Crabtree: title page, front endpages p. 2 (left middle, left bottom, top right), p. 3 (all), rear endpages p. 1 (bottom left, bottom right), p. 2 (top, bottom left), p. 3 (left middle, left bottom), p. 4 (top), p. 5 (left), p. 14 (both), p. 17, p. 22 (top), p. 23 (top), p. 26 (bottom), p. 27 (bottom), p. 28 (bottom), p. 29 (bottom), p. 31; Peter Crabtree: cover, front endpages p. 1 (all), p. 2 (top left, bottom right), rear endpages p. 1 (top left, top middle, and top right), p. 2 (bottom right), p. 3 (top left, top right, bottom right), p. 4 (bottom), p. 5 (right), p. 16 (bottom), p. 18 (bottom), p. 20 (bottom), p. 23 (bottom), p. 28 (top), p. 30; Hulton/Archive: p. 7 (left), p. 8, p. 9 (left), p. 10 (left), p. 11; Peter Matthews: p. 10 (right), p. 19; North Wind Pictures: p. 6, p. 7 (right), p. 9 (top), p. 12; Richard T. Nowitz: p. 18 (top); Tom O'Brien/International Stock: p. 15; Kay Shaw Photography: p. 24 (left); Tim Thompson: p. 26 (top), p. 27 (top)

Illustrations
Dianne Eastman: icon
David Wysotski, Allure Illustrations: back cover

Cover: A student from St. Michael's School in Dublin wears a uniform, a tradition with many schools in Ireland.

Title page: A mom escorts her children to school in Belfast.

Icon: A cottage, with plaster walls and a roof made from thatched, or woven, grasses appears at the head of each section.

Back cover: Irish hares can most often be seen at night eating grasses and chewing at young trees with their large front teeth.

Published by
Crabtree Publishing Company

PMB 16A,
350 Fifth Avenue
Suite 3308
New York
N.Y. 10118

612 Welland Avenue
St. Catharines
Ontario, Canada
L2M 5V6

73 Lime Walk
Headington
Oxford OX3 7AD
United Kingdom

Cataloging in Publication Data
Banting, Erinn,
Ireland the people / Erinn Banting.
p.cm. -- (The lands, peoples, and cultures series)
Includes bibliographical references and index.
ISBN 0-7787-9350-8 (RLB) -- ISBN 0-7787-9718-X (pbk.)
1. Ireland--Social life and customs--Juvenile literature. [1. Social life and customs.] I.Title. II. Series.
DA959.1.B36 2002
941.5--dc21
2001007748
LC

Contents

Ireland's people share a history of ancient traditions, battles, and hardships. The island they live on is divided. In the north is Northern Ireland, a province of the **United Kingdom**. In the south is the Republic of Ireland, or Éire, which is an **independent** country. For many years, the Irish have been separated by religious and political differences. While many people in Northern Ireland want to remain part of the United Kingdom, many others there and in the Republic want to be united as one country.

(left) Gaelic football is played at Croke Park in Dublin. These three boys are on their way to the stadium to cheer for their favorite team from Kerry.

(top) Most schools in Ireland require students to wear uniforms. Many uniforms include a blazer and even a tie.

(above) At one time, cricket was banned in Ireland because it was considered a British sport. Today, it is played throughout Ireland.

A changing land

In Gaelic, one of the official languages of the Republic of Ireland, *fáilte* means "welcome." Today, the Irish are welcoming many changes to their land as they work to resolve their differences. Trade, business, and employment are increasing and attracting **immigrants** from many countries. As well, the **descendants** of Irish people who were forced to leave their homeland because of hardship and war are returning to Ireland to rediscover their **heritage** and begin a new life.

Ireland's scenic country roads make cycling a popular sport. This father and son train for an upcoming race.

Early settlers

People have lived in Ireland for thousands of years. The earliest known settlers were the **Mesolithic** people, who migrated to Ireland from what is now the United Kingdom and Europe around 7000 B.C. These people survived by hunting wild boar, fishing, and gathering food such as hazelnuts. **Archaeologists** have found stone tools and other evidence of the Mesolithic people along the northern and eastern coasts of Ireland.

The **Neolithic** people, who came from the same regions as the Mesolithic people, arrived in Ireland around 3500 B.C. They settled on the coasts, but eventually moved inland, where they grew crops and raised **livestock**. In the 1960s, archaeologists discovered traces of an early Neolithic settlement in Cookstown, a town in Northern Ireland. Among their discoveries were the remains of a wooden house that was more than 5,200 years old.

The Celts

Over the next 4,000 years, many different peoples came to Ireland, but few were as powerful as the Celts. The Celts, or the Gaels as they called themselves, began coming to Ireland from Europe in 300 B.C. They divided the land into plots that individuals or families owned. These plots were grouped into small communities called *tuatha*. A *rí*, or king, ruled each *tuatha*. By around 200 A.D., all the *tuatha* were united under one *ard-rí*, or high king. The *ard-rí*, ruled from a palace on the Hill of Tara, in eastern Ireland. The Hill of Tara was the first **capital** of Ireland and remained the center of power until around 1000 A.D.

In this illustration, members of a **tuatha** *carry supplies and food to the fortress where their* **rí**, *or king, lives.*

The Vikings

The Celts ruled most of Ireland until 795 A.D., when the Vikings, a powerful group of warriors, arrived from Scandinavia. By 835, the Vikings had invaded most of the island. They destroyed settlements belonging to the Celts, stole their land, and murdered many people. Eventually, the Vikings established their own settlements along the coasts. Some of these settlements are now large cities, such as Dublin and Limerick. The Vikings introduced a new language to Ireland, called Old Norse, as well as new laws and a system of currency, or money, which replaced the **barter system**.

(below) Brian Boru introduced hereditary surnames to Ireland. Most of these names began with "O" or "Mac," which means "son of" or "descendant of." These surnames link the Irish people to their ancestors.

(above) The Vikings came to Ireland in large battleships from Scandinavia.

Brian Boru

In 1002, the Irish Celts made Brian Boru their high king. Boru thought that Ireland would be stronger as one kingdom instead of several smaller, independent kingdoms. He dissolved the old system of *tuatha* and united the Irish under one ruler. In 1014, he led the Irish army to Clontarf, near Dublin, to fight the Vikings, who controlled much of Ireland at the time. Although Boru was 74 years old, he wanted to lead the troops into battle, but his son persuaded him to stay in his tent. During the Battle of Clontarf, a Viking entered the tent and killed Boru. Even without their leader, the Irish defeated the Vikings and regained control over much of their land.

Norman rule

Normans were the descendants of Vikings who settled in France and gradually took control of Europe and England in the late 1000s and early 1100s. In 1171, the Norman king Henry II declared himself king of Ireland. He divided Irish land among English **nobles**, who built large, **fortified** castles to protect their families and possessions.

With King Henry VIII as the head of the church and state, the people of England and later Ireland were no longer under the control of the pope and the Roman Catholic Church.

By the 1300s, the Normans ruled almost all of Ireland from England. The Irish, who were mostly descendants of the Celts, **rebelled** against the Norman English nobles who had taken over their land, and slowly regained control of the island. By the 1400s, the English only governed a small part of Ireland near Dublin, known as "the Pale."

Henry VIII and the conquest

In the late 1400s, Henry VIII came to power in England and declared himself king of Ireland. He took land from the Irish, and introduced laws that removed their rights. The Irish were no longer allowed to own land or vote. He also imposed a religion called Protestantism on England and Ireland.

Protestantism

For thousands of years, Roman Catholicism was the main religion in Europe. Roman Catholicism is a **denomination** of Christianity. Christians follow the teachings of Jesus Christ, who they believe is the son of God.

In the 1500s, Catholics began to question the power of the pope, who led the Roman Catholic Church. King Henry VIII made Protestantism, another denomination of Christianity, England's official religion and declared himself the head of the country's Protestant Church, the Church of England.

Protestantism in Ireland

Between 1534 and 1537, King Henry VIII tried to force Roman Catholics in Ireland to give up their religion and follow Protestantism. He created the Church of Ireland, a branch of the Church of England. Some Irish Catholics refused to convert, or change their religion, and practiced Roman Catholicism in secret. Henry VIII punished these people by taking any land that they had won back or forcing them to work on land occupied by English **landlords**. The loss of Irish land ownership worsened the fighting between the Irish and English.

The plantations

England wanted to **colonize** Ireland by settling Protestant families, who were loyal to England, in Ireland. In 1553, Henry VIII's daughter, Mary, became the queen of England. Queen Mary sent more English people to Ireland to take over Roman Catholics' land. The new English settlements in the north and central parts of the country were called plantations because the English were "planted" on land that once belonged to the Irish. Although Catholics in Ireland rebelled, England gained control of most of the land in the north of Ireland between 1603 and 1625, when King James I planted people from Scotland.

Between 1603 and 1625, England's King James I "planted" people from Scotland in Ireland. In this illustration, an Irish family is forced to leave their farm on land that was taken over by the English.

Oliver Cromwell

In 1641, a war between Catholics and Protestants broke out in the north of Ireland, in the region known as Ulster. Catholic rebels from southern Ireland fought and killed many English and Scottish Protestants and forced many more off the Ulster plantations. The war continued for more than ten years. While the fighting in Ireland was going on, the English Parliament, led by Oliver Cromwell, defeated Charles I, England's king at the time. Cromwell sent 20,000 soldiers to Dublin to battle the Irish rebels and recapture land that was occupied by Catholics.

James II and William of Orange

The **persecution** of Irish Roman Catholics lasted until 1685, when James II, who was Roman Catholic, became the king of England and Ireland. James II tried to restore the rights of the Irish. The leaders of the Church of England and some members of the English government disagreed with James II's ideas. They took away his power, claiming that he was unfit to rule. In 1688, William of Orange, who was Protestant, became king of England and Ireland.

In 1652, Oliver Cromwell created a law called the Act of Settlement. The Act of Settlement allowed the English to take land away from Irish landowners who resisted English rule.

The Battle of the Boyne

James II did not want to give up his crown. When William became king, James II assembled an army of French and Irish Roman Catholic supporters in Ireland. At the same time, King William assembled an army of Dutch and Irish Protestants in Ireland. On July 1, 1690, the two armies fought each other on the banks of the River Boyne. The battle came to be known as the Battle of the Boyne. James II's troops lost that battle, and James II fled to France. More battles were waged over the next year. In the end, the Protestant army defeated the Catholic army.

The Penal Laws

In 1695, King William passed the Penal Laws, a set of rules to punish uncooperative Irish Catholics. Again, Irish Catholics were not allowed to vote or hold public office, their children were not allowed to attend Roman Catholic schools, and they were not allowed to own land. Many Irish Roman Catholics also suffered from poverty because they were not hired for well-paying jobs.

Daniel O'Connell, or "The Liberator," founded the Roman Catholic Association, which fought for the rights of Roman Catholics. He was the first Irish Roman Catholic to hold a seat in the British House of Commons, in 1829, after many of the Penal Laws were removed.

Each July, many Irish Protestants who support Northern Ireland's union with England march in parades. The parades take place on July 12 throughout Northern Ireland and in northern parts of the Republic. They celebrate King William's victory over James II in the Battle of the Boyne in 1690.

The Great Famine

By 1829, many of the Penal Laws had been removed and Catholics were once again allowed to vote and hold public office. Conditions slowly improved for the Irish, until 1845, when the potato crops suffered from a blight, or disease, which caused them to rot in the ground. Potatoes had been a main part of the Irish diet, especially in the south where they were the only food eaten by one-third of the population. The Irish called the resulting **famine** *an gorta mór,* which means "the great hunger."

The impact of the famine was felt less in the more industrialized north because people there could afford to buy food that was brought from England. Also, farmers in the north grew oats, which people could use to make porridge. Unfortunately, instead of extra oats being shipped to feed people starving in the south, the oats were sent to England. By 1852, 1.5 million Irish died of starvation and diseases caused by not getting enough healthy food. Another million Irish moved to the United States, Canada, and countries in Europe.

Struggle for independence

For years after the Great Famine, political, social, and economic conditions were very poor in southern Ireland. In the north, industries, such as shipbuilding, continued to grow and the economic conditions improved. People in the south, who were tired of suffering for so many years, began to demand the right to run their own country.

Sinn Féin

In 1905, an Irish journalist named Arthur Griffith founded the first Catholic **nationalist** group in Ireland. The group was called *Sinn Féin*, which means "ourselves alone" in Gaelic. *Sinn Féin* promised to fight for the rights of Irish Roman Catholics. Support for the group grew very quickly.

Smoke rises from the rubble of a building that was destroyed during the Easter Rising in Dublin in 1916.

The Easter Rising

On Easter Monday, 1916, members of various nationalist groups, including the Irish Republican Brotherhood (IRB), started a rebellion in Dublin. The nationalist groups fought against British troops for a week, but were defeated. Fifteen rebels, including IRB leader Padraig Pearse, were killed.

The *Dáil Éireann*

After the Easter Rising, the executions of nationalist rebels continued. This angered many Irish nationalists. In response, more Irish people began to support nationalist groups such as *Sinn Féin* and the IRB. In 1918, *Sinn Féin* won 73 seats in the British Parliament. They refused the seats and, instead, declared the first Irish parliament, the *Dáil Éireann*, in 1919. The *Dáil Éireann* also declared Ireland a republic, or independent country, and dissolved British rule in Ireland.

British soldiers set up a barricade during the Anglo-Irish War in 1919. Irish people called the soldiers the Black and Tans because of the colors of their mismatched uniforms. The British government was not prepared to send so many soldiers to Ireland, and had to use shirts, pants, and helmets from different army uniforms.

The Anglo-Irish War

The British refused to accept the independent government of Ireland, and **outlawed** *Sinn Féin* and the *Dáil Éireann*. British opposition to Irish independence started a conflict that lasted from 1919 to 1921, known as the Anglo-Irish War, or the War of Independence. The *Dáil Éireann* set up a military group called the Irish Republican Army (IRA). The IRA fought against Irish authorities who represented the British. In response, the British sent a military group, known as the Black and Tans, to Ireland to fight the IRA. Many people were killed in the fighting. To end the violence, the British introduced the Government of Ireland Act in 1920, which proposed to separate the northern and southern parts of Ireland. One year later, the Government of Ireland Act was accepted, and the Anglo-Irish Treaty was signed, ending the war.

Independence

In 1922, southern Ireland and three of Ulster's mostly Roman Catholic provinces became the Irish Free State, and gained independence from Britain. The rest of Ulster was called Northern Ireland. Britain ruled Northern Ireland, but the Irish Free State had its own government and ruled itself.

In 1932, Eamon de Valera, who had been very active in southern Ireland's struggle for independence, was made prime minister of the Irish Free State. He introduced a new **constitution** in 1937, which established southern Ireland as a sovereign, or independent, nation called Éire. By 1949, de Valera had withdrawn Éire completely from British rule to create a new country called the Republic of Ireland. He claimed that Northern Ireland should be part of the Republic.

"The troubles"

Between 1949 and 1968, Éire and Northern Ireland were relatively peaceful. In 1968, fighting broke out between Protestants and Catholics in L. Derry, a city in Northern Ireland, when a Catholic civil rights protest was banned. This outbreak began many years of fighting between the Roman Catholics and Protestants, a period known as "the troubles."

A group of Irish protesters approaches a barricade guarded by British soldiers on January 30, 1972.

"Bloody Sunday"

In 1970, Britain sent troops to Northern Ireland to end the fighting. People who welcomed the troops changed their minds after January 30, 1972, when the British army shot and killed thirteen demonstrators who were protesting in L. Derry. The incident became known as "Bloody Sunday." Following Bloody Sunday, violence increased in Northern Ireland. During the year, 467 people, who were mostly innocent bystanders, were killed, often by bombs placed in cars and buildings. In 2000, it was estimated that fighting in Northern Ireland since Bloody Sunday had killed more than 3,600 people and injured more than 36,000.

Ireland today

Although violence continues today, the governments of both the Republic of Ireland and the United Kingdom have taken steps to create peace in Northern Ireland. The Belfast Agreement, also known as the Good Friday Agreement, was signed by Irish and British governments in 1998. The agreement allows local governments in Northern Ireland to control education and local laws. The Belfast Agreement also states that all violent groups must give up their weapons in a move to end **terrorist** acts.

The people of both the Republic of Ireland and Northern Ireland voted overwhelmingly to accept the Belfast Agreement. It was the first time since 1918 that both the Republic of Ireland and Northern Ireland participated in the same vote. In 1999, changes were made to the Republic's constitution. For example, the Republic, which had said that Northern Ireland should be part of its country, withdrew its claim.

Mary Robinson

Mary Robinson was Ireland's first female president. She served as the seventh president of the Republic of Ireland from 1990 to 1997. As president, she worked very hard to improve life for the people of the Republic by raising their standard of living, creating new jobs, and encouraging people to end the violence in Northern Ireland. Robinson has been a role model for many young Irish people looking for peace between people of different religions because she is a Roman Catholic who married a Protestant. In 1997, Mary Robinson left Ireland to work for the United Nations. Today, she fights for the rights of people around the world.

Mary Robinson arrives in Belfast to give a speech about Irish unity.

Ireland's people

The people of Ireland and the descendants of those who left during difficult times are very proud of their heritage. They feel a deep connection to their land, especially to the county, or district, from which they come. If you ask people from Ireland where they live, they are more likely to name the county than their town or village.

The Irish

Many people who live in Ireland trace their **ancestry** back to the Celts and Vikings. The descendants of these people celebrate their roots by telling stories from Celtic and Viking folklore, playing Celtic music, creating Celtic artwork, and participating in Celtic festivals. Some people of Celtic descent live in areas of the Republic of Ireland called *Gaeltachts*, where they speak only Gaelic, the language of the Celts.

The English

Most people who are not of Celtic or Viking ancestry are descendants of the English. After the 1100s, people from England who moved to Ireland married Celts and had children. The descendants of these families are known as the Anglo-Irish. Some Anglo-Irish families still live in homes that their ancestors have owned for hundreds of years.

(above) Many children in Ireland help out on family farms after school and on weekends.

(left) A man wearing a traditional wool cap and knitted sweater takes a rest after a long day working in the fields.

14

The Ulster Scots

The descendants of the Scots who were planted in, or sent to, Ireland between 1603 and 1625 still live in Ulster today. In some areas of Belfast, where there are many people of Scottish descent, street signs are in English and Scottish Gaelic. Scottish Gaelic is a dialect, or version, of Gaelic that is spoken in Scotland.

The Travelers

Travelers, who are sometimes called Gypsies, are a people who traditionally traveled through Ireland's countryside in groups. They moved from place to place in horse-drawn carriages or brightly colored wagons, called caravans. They earned money by sharpening knives and fixing pots, pans, and kettles for people in the towns where they stopped.

Some Travelers still cross the country, but instead of using carriages or wagons, they have brightly colored trailers and pickup trucks. Other Travelers live in small settlements in rural areas throughout Northern Ireland and the Republic, where they keep their customs and traditions alive. Still others have permanently settled in cities, such as Dublin.

The Irish abroad

Descendants of Irish emigrants have influenced the world. American presidents Andrew Jackson, John F. Kennedy, Richard Nixon, and Bill Clinton were of Irish descent. John F. Kennedy, elected in 1961, was the first Roman Catholic president of the United States. President Kennedy's attitude toward people's rights in the United States gave hope to Catholics who were struggling for their rights in Ireland.

Another famous Irish-American was Henry Ford. In 1903, he started the Ford Motor Company, one of the leading car manufacturers in the world. Other famous Americans with Irish ancestors include Georgia O'Keeffe, a 20th-century painter; Frank McCourt, an author whose book *Angela's Ashes* tells about growing up in Ireland; and Harry "Bing" Crosby, a singer and actor.

A Traveler peeks out of his caravan near Galway, where he has settled for the night.

 # Life in the cities

In recent years, large cities such as Dublin and Belfast have grown very quickly. New jobs in industries such as chemical and car manufacturing are bringing people to the cities from Ireland's rural areas, from Europe, and from other parts of the world, including the United States and Canada.

Working in the cities

People in cities often work for the government or in service industries, such as tourism and sales. Other people have manufacturing jobs, working in traditional industries such as shipbuilding or in new industries such as manufacturing medicines and plastics. Limerick, in southern Ireland, is one of the fastest-growing cities in the world. Thousands of people have come to Limerick to work for computer manufacturers, such as Dell from the United States, that opened businesses there.

Along with fresh fruit and vegetables, the Moore Street Market, in downtown Dublin, offers freshly cut flowers.

(top) City Hall Park, in downtown Belfast, is a favorite place for taking a break at the end of a busy day.

Old and new

Even though Ireland's cities are growing and becoming more modern, many places still have old sections, where shops and houses line narrow cobblestone streets. In some places, the streets are so narrow that two cars cannot pass one another.

There are shopping centers and apartment buildings in the modern areas, but only a few large office complexes and skyscrapers. City governments rarely allow anyone to construct tall buildings to preserve the history of the area. In Dublin, it is very difficult to get a permit to construct a building that is more than seven stories high.

"The bunkers"

Sometimes, when tall buildings are built in historic areas, there is disagreement. On Wood Quay, a street in northern Dublin, are two buildings called "the bunkers."

During the 1950s, part of an ancient Viking settlement and part of the wall that surrounded Dublin hundreds of years ago were discovered on the site where the bunkers now stand. After years of protest from the people of Dublin, the city allowed the bunkers to be constructed on top of the archaeological site. Today, the ruins can no longer be seen. To honor the historic site, a plaque hangs in the lobby of one of the buildings, and a picnic area in the shape of a Viking ship was constructed outside.

Culture in the cities

Music, dance, film, and art are important to the people of Ireland. Cities such as Cork and Dublin hold annual jazz and film festivals that attract visitors from all over the world. Festivals, such as the International Choral and Folk Dance Festival in Cork, present traditional Celtic music and dancing.

The statue of Daniel O'Connell dominates a Dublin intersection. O'Connell's peaceful pursuit of Irish rights made him a hero in Ireland. He helped bring in a new law that allowed Catholics to vote.

Life in the countryside

Small towns and villages dot Ireland's green farmland. Each community developed around a central square long ago. Today, farmers and other people who live on the outskirts of towns and villages meet in the central square to socialize, hold town meetings, and do business.

Working on a farm

Most people in the countryside make their living from farming. Farmers wake up very early to feed livestock, milk cows, put animals in the pasture to graze, and tend crops. Children who live on farms often help with the daily chores before and after school. In the evenings, after the work is done, many farmers ride to town to visit the public house, or pub. A pub is a place where people eat, drink, and meet with friends.

A farmer rests next to his tractor, which is loaded with a bail of hay. The hay will be used to feed his cows and sheep.

A farmer and his sheepdog check on the sheep.

Puck Fair is a popular harvest festival. During the fair, people dress up in colorful costumes and parade a goat, called "the king of the fair," through the streets.

Harvest time

In the fall, after the crops are harvested, small towns and villages celebrate with festivals. Lammas Day, on August 1, is a popular harvest festival. One of the most famous Lammas Day celebrations takes place in Ballycastle, a town in Northern Ireland. People set up stalls where they sell a variety of goods, including food, clothing, and even horses. A favorite part of Lammas Day in Ballycastle is eating the town's famous treats — *duileasc*, which is a red seaweed, and yellowman, a sweet, crunchy toffee.

Homes

Small, one-story houses made of plaster or stone walls and thatched roofs once lined the streets of towns and villages. The thatched roofs, which were made from straw or tightly woven grasses, kept out the rain and kept in the heat. Today, some of these houses still stand. People who live in these homes often use peat to heat them. Peat, which comes from **bogs**, is a rich soil made up of decaying plants.

The church

The church is an important part of life in Ireland where nine out of ten people go every Sunday. In rural areas, it is the center of many events and social activities. After church, people stay to chat with their friends, neighbors, and relatives. The church also organizes dinners, dances, and fairs for the community.

Blow-ins

Many young people in Ireland's rural areas move to cities to find jobs and to experience city life. They often sell land that they **inherited** to people from other parts of the world, such as Europe. The new immigrants often fall in love with the Irish countryside and those who live there. The newcomers renovate the old homes, raise families, and open businesses. Local Irish people call them "blow-ins" because they are like seeds that blow across the water and into Ireland.

Family celebrations

Visiting family and friends is just one way to spend leisure time. These cousins get together every month.

Irish children celebrate their birthdays with gifts, games, and parties. A large meal, a birthday cake, ice cream, and the bumps are all part of the fun. With the bumps, a person is held by the arms and legs and bumped gently on the ground for each year of his or her birthday. Shrieks of laughter and excitement can be heard during games such as tag, which is called "tig" in Ireland. People also call out *"Bretithlá Sona!"* which is Gaelic for "Happy birthday!" Another common birthday wish is *"Go maire tú an céad!"* or "May you live to be 100!"

Getting engaged

When a couple in Ireland gets engaged, it is considered good luck for the man to give the woman a ring with her birthstone in it. The good luck will continue if the couple chooses the right month and day for the wedding.

The Irish believe that December is a very lucky month, while May is very unlucky. A well-known rhyme gives advice about when people should marry: "Monday for wealth; Tuesday for health; Wednesday, the best day of all; Thursday for crosses; Friday for losses; and Saturday, no day at all." Christmas Day and New Year's Day are lucky days for a wedding, no matter what day of the week they fall on.

The big day

Many superstitions about weddings involve the wedding day. At some weddings, a small boy or girl who takes part in the wedding ceremony presents the bride and groom with a silver horseshoe, so the couple will have good fortune. If the bride accidentally tears her wedding dress, it is also considered good luck.

Many Irish people believe that if the sun shines on a bride on her wedding day, she and her husband will be lucky for the rest of their marriage.

Mí na meala

The familiar word "honeymoon" has roots in Irish superstition. During the Middle Ages, between 476 A.D. and 1453 A.D., Irish **monks** made a honey drink called mead. The mead was used as medicine. After two people married, they were given enough mead to last for one month. People thought the medicine protected the bride from evil fairies who wanted to take her away. In Gaelic, the month was called *mí na meala*, which means "the month of honey." People now refer to the time after a wedding as a "honeymoon."

The *bean sí*

One of the most famous Irish superstitions is about a spirit, called the *bean sí*, or banshee. People believe that the banshee cries outside a person's home before his or her death to warn the family.

Today, some Irish people celebrate a person's death with a wake, but more people have a church service without the traditional wake.

Gathering for a wake

In Ireland, people think of death as the start of a new life. A person's death is not always a sad occasion, but a time for celebration. In the past, the family and friends of a person who died gathered in someone's home for a very elaborate wake. The wake often lasted several days. The body was laid out in a coffin in the living room so people could see it and pay their respects. People also prayed, told stories, sang, and even played games to honor the person who died.

Wakes began in Ireland to prevent people from being buried alive. During the Great Famine, before wakes were performed, many Irish died and were buried quickly. Sometimes, people who were very ill looked like they were dead and were buried by mistake. When their coffins were opened to lay another body inside, people sometimes found scratches from the dead person's fingernails, which meant that the person had been buried alive and was trying to get out. Three-day wakes allowed family and friends to make sure that their loved one was dead, and would not "wake" after being buried.

Time to eat!

The kitchen was once the center of daily life for most Irish families. Not only was it where people ate, it was also where children slept. Families built an alcove, or small area, beside the warm stove where a child's bed could fit.

Today, after a long day at work or school, many Irish families still gather in the kitchen to talk and enjoy a meal together. Sometimes, they eat traditional dishes, such as Irish stew or fish and chips. Foods from other countries, such as pizza, hamburgers, and Chinese food, are becoming popular as well.

(below) A woman displays the many dishes she has made using traditional Irish ingredients, such as potatoes, cabbage, fish, and meat.

(above) Moore Market, in Dublin, is one of the many outdoor markets where people can buy fresh fruit and vegetables.

Butchers in Northern Ireland and the Republic sell fresh beef, lamb, and pork, which comes from livestock raised on farms throughout the island.

Mealtime

One hundred years ago, most people in Ireland enjoyed a large breakfast early in the morning, a main meal in the middle of the day, and a lighter meal at the end of the day. Usually, breakfast, called a fry, consisted of two fried eggs, bacon or sausages, grilled tomatoes, brown bread, juice, and tea. Most people lived on farms, and they needed a large breakfast to give them energy for their morning's work. At lunchtime, they enjoyed another big meal that included meat, potatoes, and bread. The evening meal, called tea, was smaller. It included mashed, boiled, or baked potatoes, vegetables, and bread. Today, most people eat smaller breakfasts and lunches, and enjoy larger meals at the end of the day.

Pickled and salted foods

During the Great Famine, the Irish found ways to preserve the little food they had. Vegetables, such as cabbage, sugar beets, and onions, were pickled, or stored in vinegar or brine, a type of salty water. Meat was salted, or soaked in a salty solution, and then dried. Today, the Irish still pickle foods and salt meat, even though they have refrigerators to keep their food fresh, because they like the taste.

Irish stew

Irish stew is a popular dish that is most often made with meat, such as beef or lamb, and vegetables, such as potatoes, carrots, and onions. Some people add other ingredients and cook the stew in different ways. Dublin coddle, which is corned beef and cabbage, is a favorite type of Irish stew. Meat, potatoes, cabbage, carrots, and onions are all boiled in a large pot. Once all the ingredients are cooked, the meat and vegetables are removed and covered in a sauce made from mayonnaise or horseradish and a lot of spices.

People traditionally made Irish stew because they wanted to put all their ingredients into the same dish. The stew was healthy, easy to make, and often lasted for more than one meal.

Carrageen moss

Carrageen moss, called *cairrgín* in Gaelic, is an Irish specialty. The reddish-brown plant grows on rocks and in shallow pools along the shores of western Ireland. People began eating it during the Great Famine, when they had little else to eat. Carrageen moss is washed, dried, and boiled until it becomes a jelly. The jelly is used in soups, stews, and puddings. Many people believe that Carrageen moss prevents certain diseases and cures people who are sick.

Bread

The Irish bake breads using the same recipes that their ancestors used hundreds of years ago. Soda bread is a favorite food in both Northern Ireland and the Republic, although it is made differently in each place. In Northern Ireland, people call soda bread "farl." They shape the dough into a circle, then cut it into four pieces and prepare it in a frying pan on top of a stove. In the Republic of Ireland, people call soda bread "cake." It has the same ingredients as farl, but has a flat, round shape. A cross is cut into the top of it before it is baked in the oven.

To make soda bread, flour, eggs, buttermilk or sour milk, salt, sugar, and baking soda are combined. The milk and baking soda make the bread rise.

Many people serve champ with meat, such as beef, lamb, or pork, and other vegetables, such as carrots, peas, or cabbage.

"Spuds"

Potatoes, or "spuds" as they are called in Ireland, are the most important part of any Irish meal. One of the easiest and quickest ways to cook potatoes is to make champ. You can make champ with an adult's help.

What you need:
• 8 medium-sized potatoes, peeled and cut into quarters
• a pot
• water
• a potato masher
• 6 scallions or green onions, chopped
• 2 1/2 cups (625 ml) milk
• pepper and salt to taste
• 4 tablespoons (60 ml) butter

Fill the pot with enough water to cover the potatoes, and bring the water to a boil. Add salt, and boil the potatoes for 20 to 30 minutes, until they are soft. Drain the water and mash the potatoes. Add the onions, milk, salt, and pepper. Mash the potatoes until they are fluffy. Form the champ into small mounds and scoop out the center. Drop a bit of butter into the center and serve.

Chippers

Chip vans, or chippers, are stands and trucks that sell fish and chips by the side of the road in Ireland's cities. The fish, such as cod or sole, is dipped in a thick batter, fried, and served with French fries. People can also order a popular Irish treat called a chip butty from a chipper. A chip butty is a sandwich made from a roll, called a bap, butter, French fries, and ketchup or mayonnaise. Chippers also sell other foods fried in batter, such as hamburgers, sausages, and even candy bars!

Drink up!

People around the world drink Irish whiskey and Irish beer. Irish whiskey is made with barley, a grain that grows throughout the country. The grain is malted, or soaked until it sprouts, then dried and smoked over a fire. This gives whiskey a smoky flavor. Hot water is then added to the barley, which then soaks until it produces a liquid called wort. The wort is placed in large barrels, called casks, and aged until it becomes alcohol.

Irish beer

Beer is also made from barley, at a factory called a malthouse. After the barley is ground in a mill, it is mixed with water, mashed, and added to hops. Hops are dried flowers from the hop vine. They make beer taste less bitter and keep it from spoiling. The mixture of barley and hops is then boiled in a large pot called a copper and stored in casks.

Guinness

A famous kind of beer has been made in Dublin since 1759. Guinness beer was originally made by Arthur Guinness. He developed a beer that was stronger, darker, and did not spoil as quickly as other types of beer. Today, Guinness is one of the largest companies in Ireland, and Guinness beer is served all over the world.

Friends toast one another at a pub in Dublin by saying "sláinte" which is a Gaelic word that means "cheers."

Sports and leisure

Rain or shine, the people of Ireland enjoy many outdoor activities and sports, including walking, gardening, boating, golfing, and fishing. They also get together to play darts and cards, or to play music and sing in their homes or local pubs.

Soccer

Soccer, or "football" as it is called in Ireland, is the most popular sport. Children and adults play soccer with their friends after work or school. Some join a soccer league, where they compete against other teams in their region. During the World Cup, an international soccer tournament that takes place every four years, Irish soccer fans are glued to the television or radio, cheering for their country's team.

Gaelic football

Gaelic football is a special type of soccer. Each team has fifteen players who try to kick a ball, similar to a soccer ball, through the other team's goal posts. Players can touch the ball with their hands, and pass the ball from their feet to their hands while running. Gaelic football is much rougher than soccer, and players often get hurt.

These boys are playing soccer, or football as they call it, during recess.

To score a goal in hurling, players have to get the ball through the other team's goal posts. The goal posts are shaped like the letter H. If players get the ball over the crossbar, they score one point. If they hit the ball under the crossbar, their team scores three points.

Hurling

The ancient game of *iomáin,* or hurling, dates back to 1200 B.C. and is still played throughout Ireland. A player hits a ball across a field with a long stick, called a *camán* or hurley, or carries the ball on the *camán's* crooked blade. The ball, called a *sliothar,* is made of cork wound with wool and covered in leather, like a baseball.

Off to the races

Going to the races is a favorite Irish pastime. People crowd around racetracks to watch greyhounds, a type of dog, or horses race. Some of the fastest horses in the world come from Ireland, and more than 300 races take place there every year. One of the largest races is the Irish Derby. It is held each year in Kildare, a town in eastern Ireland.

Riders warm up at a steeplechase course before a tournament in Ballsbridge, a town in the eastern Republic.

Steeplechase

Steeplechase is another popular Irish sport involving horses. It began in 1752, when two men on horseback raced each other across the countryside. The horses jumped over hedges, walls, and ditches. The sport got its name from the tall church steeples that racers used as landmarks so they knew in which direction to go. Steeplechase races are now run on a course, with riders and their horses jumping over obstacles.

Road bowling

In certain parts of Ireland, such as County Cork in the south, people play a game called road bowling. Road bowling is similar to regular bowling, but it is played on a country road with a very heavy ball made from cast iron. Players mark out an area about two miles (four kilometers) long. Each player throws the ball along the road until it reaches the finish line. The person who gets the ball over the finish line in the fewest number of throws wins.

(below) Ireland is known world-wide for breeding and training winning race horses. Many prize horses from Ireland race in North America.

(above) These three school girls must pass through Dublin's busy downtown to get to school each day.

(below) Students learn a variety of subjects in grade school. In the Republic, all students must learn the Gaelic language as well as English.

In Ireland, all children attend school from the age of four or five to sixteen. Most schools look similar to schools in North American cities. In parts of the countryside where few people live, some schoolhouses have only one or two rooms, and students of different ages learn together. Children in these areas who are older than twelve often take buses to secondary schools in nearby towns or cities.

Time to study

Children in Northern Ireland and the Republic study many of the same subjects, such as math, science, history, art, music, and English. Children in the Republic also study Gaelic.

School systems

At the age of twelve, students in the Republic go to secondary school. There are two types of secondary schools. At secondary technical schools, students study subjects such as math, science, English, Gaelic, and history. At vocational schools, they also learn a skill, such as woodworking or computer programming. At the age of fifteen, all students take a difficult exam called the junior certificate. Many students who pass this exam continue school for another two years, and then take more exams. Once they pass these exams, they receive their "Leaving Certificate" and go on to university or begin a job.

When children in Northern Ireland are sixteen years old, they take an exam in each subject they studied. There are two types of exams — the GCSE, or General Certificate in Secondary Education, and A-level exams, which are more difficult. Students who pass their GCSE earn a general certificate. This means they can continue in secondary school, go to a college, or leave school and begin working. Students who pass their A-level exams attend two more years of secondary school and then can go to university.

Religious education

In the Republic of Ireland, all children used to go to schools that were run by the Roman Catholic Church. Religion was an important part of their education. Today, more children of different backgrounds go to schools where they study not only Roman Catholicism, but also many other religions, including Protestantism, Judaism, and Islam. These schools are run by the government, not by the church.

Integrated schools

For many years, Roman Catholics in Northern Ireland did not go to the same schools as Protestants. Often, the two groups lived in separate neighborhoods because of political differences. Children went to school with other children in their neighborhood, who were of the same religion. Today, there are integrated primary and secondary schools in Northern Ireland, where children from different religions and backgrounds attend classes together.

Trinity College Dublin, or TCD, was founded by Queen Elizabeth I in 1592 and is Ireland's oldest university.

Some students who decide to work after secondary school do apprenticeships, where they are taught a skill, such as shipbuilding.

Exchanges

In order for students in Northern Ireland and the Republic of Ireland to learn about each other, schools in some cities pair up. Students from a class in the Republic correspond with students from a class in Northern Ireland. They write letters and e-mails to each other, work on projects together, and have videoconferences so they can see and talk to one another using computers. Some classes even meet in person to have a party and get to know one another better.

Shelagh lives with her brother and parents in an apartment in Dublin.

Most mornings, Shelagh's mother has to wake her up, but not today! Shelagh can't wait to get to school and finally meet her friend Brian during a videoconference. So far, Shelagh and Brian have only e-mailed one another.

Brian goes to the Gilnahirk Primary School in Belfast. Shelagh lives in Dublin and goes to the North Dublin National School Project. Shelagh's class and Brian's class participate in a project that pairs schools from Northern Ireland and the Republic of Ireland, so that students like Shelagh and Brian can get to know one another.

"Shelagh," her mother calls, "you're going to miss your bus if you don't hurry up and eat your breakfast!"

Shelagh runs down the hallway of the apartment where she and her family live. Shelagh's father, who has already eaten his breakfast, pours her a cup of tea.

"Do you want one egg or two?" Shelagh's mother asks as Shelagh pours sugar into her tea.

"I feel like a gentleman this morning!" Shelagh laughs. Many people in Ireland still call a breakfast with one egg a lady's fry and a breakfast with two eggs a gentleman's fry, although most people don't eat very large breakfasts like they used to. Shelagh is so excited that she is sure she can eat two eggs this morning.

When Shelagh gets to school, the class's computer is all set up. Each class at the two schools has a special computer with a camera and microphone in it, so the children can see and hear each other.

"Class, get your poems and gather around. We're almost ready," Miss O'Connell says. Shelagh and Brian had to work on a project together. They read a book called *Under the Hawthorne Tree* about a woman named Elsa who lived in Ireland during the Great Famine, and they each wrote a poem about the story. During the videoconference, they'll discuss the book, read their poems to one another, and ask each other questions about where they live.

Miss O'Connell types the number for the Gilnahirk Primary School into the computer. "Here they are," she says, as a picture of the class pops up on the computer screen.

Brian looks up information about **Under the Hawthorne Tree** *to use in his poem. He is excited to show his work over the Internet to Shelagh and her classmates.*

Mrs. Ross and her P7 class smile and wave at Miss O'Connell's class. Even though students in Shelagh's class and Brian's class are the same age, there are different names for their grades. In Northern Ireland, children who are eleven are in P7, and in the Republic of Ireland, children who are eleven are in fifth class.

After everyone settles down, the students stand in front of the computer one at a time to introduce themselves and read their poems. When they finish talking about the book, they ask questions about what it's like to live in Northern Ireland or the Republic of Ireland.

The students discover differences in their lives. In Belfast, there have been many years of fighting between Protestants and Roman Catholics. Although the violence is not as bad as it once was, some areas are still dangerous.

The students of Gilnahirk are surprised to learn that all the street signs in Dublin are written in both English and Gaelic. "We only see signs like that here in certain neighborhoods," Brian says. "We don't learn Gaelic like you do in the Republic."

The students also discover that their lives are similar in many ways. They watch the same TV programs, play the same sports — especially soccer — and eat the same foods. They all agree that "chip butties" are their favorite treat.

At the end of the videoconference, the children wave goodbye to one another. "That was a lot of fun," Shelagh says to her friend Kate. "I can't wait until next week when we do it again!"

Glossary

ancestry The people from whom one is descended

archaeologist A person who studies the past by looking at buildings and artifacts

barter system An exchange of goods or services that does not involve money

bog An area of soft, wet land

capital A city where the government of a state or country is located

colonize To establish a settlement in a distant country

constitution The set of laws that govern a country

denomination An organized religious group within a faith

descendant A person who can trace his or her family roots to a certain family or group

famine An extreme shortage of food in a country

fortified Strengthened against attacks

heritage Customs, objects, and achievements handed down from earlier generations

immigrant A person who settles in another country

independent Not governed by a foreign power

inherit To receive something from someone after he or she has died

landlord A person who owns and rents houses or land

livestock Farm animals

Mesolithic Belonging to the period between the Paleolithic and the Neolithic ages when prehumans hunted, fished, and gathered food

monk A member of a male religious community who has taken certain vows, such as silence and poverty

nationalist A person who wants his or her country to be independent

Neolithic Belonging to the period after the Mesolithic age, when prehumans used stone tools, farmed, and began pottery and weaving

noble A person born into a high social class

outlaw To make illegal

persecution The harming of another person for religious, racial, or political reasons

rebel To oppose a government or authority

terrorist Using extreme violence, often for political reasons

United Kingdom A group of countries including England, Scotland, Wales, and Northern Ireland

 # Index

A. Family life is very important in Ireland. Barbara and Brian Gallivan have five children. Left to right is Hannah (12), Gerry (9), Barbara, Katie (4), and Kevin (13).

B. Grandfather Gerry Gallivan has had one of his many plays, The Prophecy, performed at Ireland's famous Abbey Theater in Dublin.

C. Brian Gallivan, the son of Gerry, is the president of a company in Dublin. He is sitting with his son, Kevin, and his wife, Barbara.

D. Maura Gallivan (6), on the left, with two of her neighborhood friends.

E. This young family takes a rest after crossing the shaky Carrick-a-rede rope bridge in Northern Ireland.

St. Michael's School, near Dublin

A. Students from St. Michael's country school get together for a group picture at recess.

B. These girls play the Irish version of tag, called tig.

C. Mr. Neill Moynihan is the deputy principal of St. Michael's School.